Non*monogamy* **&** Defying a Paradigm

More Than Two Essentials

Non*monogamy* &
Defying a Paradigm

Marla **Schreiber**

THORNAPPLE PRESS

Nonmonogamy and Defying a Paradigm
A More Than Two Essentials Guide

Thornapple Press, 300–722 Cormorant Street
Victoria, BC V8W 1P8 Canada press@thornapplepress.ca

Our business offices are located on the traditional, ancestral and unceded territories of the lək̓ʷəŋən and W̱SÁNEĆ peoples. We return a percentage of company profits to the original stewards of this land through South Island Reciprocity Trust. Thornapple Press is a brand of Talk Science to Me Communications Inc. Talk Science is a WBE Canada Certified Women Business Enterprise, a CGLCC Certified 2SLGBTQI+-owned business, and a Certified Living Wage Employer.

Cover and interior design © 2025 by Jeffrey Werner.
Substantive editing by Andrea Zanin. Copy-editing by Hazel Boydell.
Proofreading by Heather van der Hoop.

Library and Archives Canada Cataloguing in Publication
Title: Nonmonogamy & defying a paradigm / Marla Schreiber.
Other titles: Nonmonogamy and defying a paradigm
Names: Schreiber, Marla, author.
Description: Series statement: More than two essentials ; 11 | Includes bibliographical references.
Identifiers: Canadiana (print) 20250178249 | Canadiana (ebook) 2025018141X | ISBN 9781990869761 (softcover) | ISBN 9781990869778 (EPUB) | ISBN 9781990869907 (PDF)
Subjects: LCSH: Non-monogamous relationships. | LCSH: Intimacy (Psychology)
Classification: LCC HQ980 .S37 2025 | DDC 306.84/23—dc23

10 9 8 7 6 5 4 3 2 1

Printed and bound in Canada by Marquis.

This book is dedicated to our collective courage to defy the status quo in order to live life authentically.

Contents

Acknowledgements

Writing this book has encouraged me to take stock of the fractal-like webs of community that raise me up to be the best version of myself. This process has been illuminating, challenging and most of all humbling beyond belief!

Thanks to my parents, I was offered the opportunity to be accepted as myself growing up (what a gift). I definitely felt like "the ugly duckling" in my earliest community, where I never felt like I fit in. The support at home allowed me to be unapologetically authentic, outspoken, weird (which later translated to neuro-fabulous and Queer) and nonmonogamous as I explored new communities. It took until I was in my mid-teens, surrounded by other "ugly ducklings," to realize that we didn't quite fit in with the ducks because we were *freaking swans*!

I have had the overwhelming privilege of being uplifted by elders and teachers who supported my defiant shenanigans along the way.

At school: Joel Hart (RIP) introduced me to polyamory while professors Irini Tsakiri, Penny Stewart, Ellen Moore and Dr. Raye Kass challenged me, put up with me and defended my right to be exactly as I was.

In therapy: Niyati Evers and Jen Maramba have both been teachers, guides and family to me in different ways over the years. You have both shown up in full acceptance of the entirety of my being while gently challenging me. I am a better human, partner, community member, friend, educator and therapist because of the ways you have modelled eldership for me.

At home: Bubby Bea—my grandmother—opened her swanky Montreal condo to me and my growing community of chosen family, friends, lovers and partners. Whether she was away doing the snowbird thing in Florida or living with us as roommates without judgment, she offered us all the privilege of a safe space to grow into our gawky swan necks and authentic selves.

Beyond: I am infinitely grateful to All My Relations who support me along my journey in the physical world and the worlds of Spirit. Thank you to the guardian Cedars, Maple and Spruce who protect our home in The Forest. Thank you to my animal kin and Familiars, and every Stone-friend who has taught me a lesson or agreed to come home with me. Thank you to The Elements as my teachers.

At age 14, in my earliest days of exploring new "ponds," I met Adam Bagatavicius—the fluffiest swan—in a low-budget community acting class. He was mysterious, hilarious, brilliant and authentic, and he always walked around with a notepad in hand and a guitar on his back (everyone swooned). In 2005, we fell in love by accident, and spent years crafting a Queer nonmonogamous partnership that would lay the foundation for my life's work as a nonmonogamy-focused speaker, educator, therapist and now writer. Thanks to the support of our loving interdependent relationship, I was able to be brave while exploring my own identity and new experiences because I knew that I would always be met with empathy, accountability and acceptance.

Reining in my chaos is no easy feat, and there is no one I trust more with this task than Adam. Not only has he been my life partner for over 20 years, but he is also an incredible partner at work. Everything you read in this text has been lovingly and exhaustively edited by his sharp editorial eyes (imagine if the Queen of Swords in Tarot was a copy editor).

Adam also participated in co-creating LovePlus Collective, a queer-centric community and support group for the nonmonogamous in Toronto in 2017–2018. That community led us to the current PolyaMarla "professional polycule," which supported me in getting online and creating nonmonogamy education content. They are the backbone of all the education work we've been doing since 2022. I don't know if the word "gratitude" can even sum up the way I feel toward the incredible PolyaMarla team.

@PolyaMarla is the handle I started using on social media to create content focused on nonmonogamous relationships. Were it not for my beloved online communities who show up to support and engage with my content, I don't know if I would have had the courage to apply to speak about mononormativity at the Southwest Love Fest conference in 2024. By showing up in *that* community, I was able to connect with Eve Rickert, who casually offered me the opportunity to write this book.

Thank you so much to the whole team at Thornapple Press who have been so patient and loving with my wild heart and deadline aversions. Special thanks to Eve Rickert for taking a chance on me, to Andrea

Zanin for ferociously editing my chaos and to Hazel Boydell for the finishing touches and deep well of patience.

I am one person who has been and continues to be raised up by the interlocking hands of communities that have accepted and included me. I aim to give thanks for every opportunity that has come my way by helping to raise others up in kind.

I cannot even begin to express my gratitude for all the people who have trusted me as a therapist and educator over the years. Please know that everyone I work with in any of these capacities is also my teacher. Our growth is inextricably linked, and I am better at my job and my life because of the people who invest in my wisdom and growth. Whether you've left me a question or comment online, attended one of my groups or workshops, or joined me as a counterpart in the therapeutic alliance, I would not be who I am today without you!

On a more personal note, I could never support others on their nonmonogamy journeys if friends, partners, lovers and Queer platonic relations had not taken a shot at loving me. To my beloved Michelle, thank you for co-creating this magical thing we've got going on for so many years. Thank you for giving me a reason to smile every time I see the moon looking down at me from the sky. Your brilliance and experience with nonmonogamy has helped me to imagine new possibilities in my own relationships.

To my Montreal fam: Thank you! Sandra, I would choose you as my sister over and over again even if we weren't related by blood! Your openness and love have known no bounds, and I don't know who I would be if you hadn't been there to boss around in our youth, and boss me around in our adulthood.

To the sweeties who continue to show me how to co-create relationship anarchy, Queer platonic relationships and relationship transitions beyond my wildest dreams: Gyp, Erin, Olivia and Zaye—I don't know where I'd be without your love and support!

To all the partners and metamours of past and present who have loved, laughed and cried together: Thank you, you're welcome, and I'm sorry.

Introduction

It's hard to stay dry in the rain.

Imagine being somewhere like Seattle or Vancouver in the wintertime, where most people hide under umbrellas or don hooded rain jackets and walk with eyes to the ground to avoid getting splashed in the face by rainfall that ranges from mist to downpour. Let's say you've been out all day in the rain and you're cold, drenched and generally uncomfortable. You head home to where you have towels, blankets and a fresh change of clothes to dry off and warm up. You drink a hot beverage and finally feel comfy and cozy… and before you know it, it's time to head back out into the rain.

Even with your best waterproof gear, you won't be able to stay dry forever. Whether it's your pants below the jacket and above the boots, or whatever parts of you are not covered by the umbrella, if you're out there for long enough, at least some of you is getting wet. (*So fun!*) This is true even though you're clearly aware of the climate and have amassed tools and strategies to keep as dry as possible.

What about someone who is visiting for the first time? What if they are unprepared for the climate and have no concept of how to navigate the rain? (Maybe they're not a big planner and haven't checked the weather in advance. Maybe they are used to a desert climate. I don't know this person but I'm sure they exist.) Obviously, this person is going to be soaked and cold as long as they're outdoors or until they accumulate the gear necessary to manage the weather conditions more effectively.

This is what it's like to try to unlearn or deconstruct a paradigm while still having to exist within it. No matter how much we may fortify ourselves with knowledge, tools, strategies and experiences so that we can stand our ground and think critically about what we've been taught, we must still face the omnipresent norms, values, expectations, laws and other factors that reinforce the paradigm's existence.

For those of us interested in shifting our worldview to practise nonmonogamy, it can be like playing a difficult video game. We find ourselves battling the "big boss" of deconstructing and unlearning everything we've been taught by the monogamous paradigm. When society positions monogamy as the normal or correct way to engage in intimate partnerships (we call this mononormativity), it stigmatizes and marginalizes anything that deviates from that norm. While we may have opportunities to savour the sweet taste of victory here and there, we also have to brace ourselves for the next levels where said boss has somehow reincarnated into a more powerful opponent.

About Marla

Hi, I'm Marla. Allow me to introduce myself.

I'm a white, Queer, gender-defiant (they/them pronouns), neuro-fabulous

(ADHD) relationship therapist and educator, with Ashkenazi Jewish settler ancestry on Turtle Island (also known as North America). I've been practising polyamory since 2005 and facilitating workshops and training on the subject in academic and professional settings since 2009.[1]

After years of focusing on my work as a sexual health and social justice educator and facilitator, I struggled with academic systems and institutions to complete a Master of Social Work in 2017. From there, I began a private therapy practice focused on supporting 2SLGBTQIA+[2] communities. However, it didn't take long before I was specializing in nonmonogamy support for individuals, couples and groups (both families and polycules[3]), where there was a clear gap in services. It was that absence of professional awareness and sensitivity to nonmonogamous relationship dynamics that began to ignite my passion and curiosity about how I could develop my work to further support nonmonogamous communities.

At the end of 2020, one of my partners and I moved to the woods outside of Tkaronto (also known as Toronto, in so-called Canada). Between the isolation from the ongoing COVID-19 pandemic and from relocating to a rural area, it didn't take long before I found myself in a place of deep grief and missing the communities that made me feel at home. I decided to create educational content on social media as @PolyaMarla to build community. While my focus has generally been on relationships and nonmonogamy, I also use my platforms to discuss topics including gender, trauma, grief, sexuality, social justice, anti-oppression, anti-racism and much more.

As my work on social media was gaining reach, I was simultaneously noticing a growing need for more nonmonogamy training and support for service providers. All too frequently I connected with people who had experienced harm at the hands of uninformed, biased and sometimes discriminatory therapists, nurses, doctors and other professionals. In response, I founded PolyaMarla Inc. in 2023. We are a little "professional polycule" of Queer, nonmonogamous folks who are committed to providing support, education and training to those practising or interested in understanding nonmonogamy.

I often say that my personal, professional and political worlds are deeply intertwined. One of my favourite parts of supporting people connected to my own communities is that I can pull from so many different areas of learning and experience and share these lessons with others. Being able to exist as my authentic self professionally and helping others to navigate the sometimes-murky waters of nonmonogamy feels like a gift.

About This Book

Having the privilege of connecting with a wide range of people internationally allows me the opportunity to notice trends and themes in the questions that come my way. In 2023, I noticed that many people were struggling with something that continues to be a challenge for me, even after two decades of practising nonmonogamy. The echoes of monogamous expectations and relational dynamics can impact the ways we approach our nonmonogamous relationships, despite our efforts to learn and employ "best practices" for nonmonogamy. Unfortunately, trying to adapt the operating system from one paradigm to another can leave us feeling stuck and frustrated, because when we shift paradigms, we also have to shift values, perspectives and behaviours.

Recognizing that unlearning a paradigm is incredibly challenging, I was inspired to offer a workshop about mononormativity at a conference. It was clear to me that I could not talk about deconstructing one paradigm without connecting it to others that coexist as part of the fabric of society. So, I tackled mononormativity while also trying to offer tools for understanding and deconstructing paradigms in general.

After that conference I reached out to a fellow participant who had caught my attention during a workshop about community care and accountability. You know when someone says something that really resonates? I was feeling a call to continue the conversation if she had capacity to engage. I hadn't realized that this person was Eve Rickert, co-author of *More Than Two* and publisher of Thornapple Press. She generously offered me the opportunity to expand the conversation about mononormativity in a book—this book! I said yes before I even fully processed the offer.

In this text, I will explain some key concepts related to nonmonogamy to develop a shared language. We will dig into the nitty-gritty of how paradigms affect our lives in general, and then zoom in on the impact that the paradigm of mononormativity has on nonmonogamous relationships. I know this can sound daunting, so I will make sure to include concrete examples to help anchor some of the more abstract concepts. I'll offer tools and strategies to explore the impact of these paradigms on our lives and reflection questions to support you along your journey of putting theory into practice.

Who Am I Talking To?

You do not have to be actively engaged in nonmonogamy to benefit from reading this book.

While I provide education focused on supporting and fostering healthy nonmonogamous relationship dynamics, *anyone* can benefit from the information and tools that I share. Most of the skills I teach are rooted in developing healthy communication and becoming attuned to ourselves and our loved ones. While I typically use examples related to non-monogamy, I often receive heartening feedback from monogamous people looking to learn and grow as individuals.

You might be a professional who is hoping to support nonmonogamous people in your work. This would be a dream for me! While this text is by no means a replacement for proper training about how to work with nonmonogamous populations, it is definitely a great way to become acquainted with some of the challenges we face and strategies for overcoming them. Perhaps you're an ally, coworker, family member or friend of someone practising nonmonogamy. I would be delighted to know that people are interested in becoming more knowledgeable about nonmonogamy as a way of normalizing these kinds of relationships, rather than fearing or stigmatizing them. Having more information about something, even if it's not our personal cup of tea, allows us to stop the spread of misinformation and to make informed decisions in our own lives.

Of course, this book is certainly also intended for anyone who is interested in or already practising nonmonogamy. You might be newer in your exploration and hoping to set a solid foundation for your relationships, or you might have been practising nonmonogamy for years. You could also be in a monogamous relationship with a partner who has shared an interest in opening up the dynamic. That can be a lot to take in and if that is the case, I hope that this text can provide you with a little more context about the work that we do to engage in nonmonogamy in a world that reflects monogamous values to us at every turn.

Whether you are seeking to understand how monogamous norms impact nonmonogamous relationships or are seeking practical tools for building healthy relationships, this book is for you.

Part I
Concepts and Definitions

The topic of mononormativity can be quite dense and cerebral.

One complex term unfolds into the next, and I realize that it can become overwhelming if we aren't all on the same page. So, let's start by breaking down some concepts and definitions. From there we can investigate the nuance of working to deconstruct mononormativity without unintentionally reproducing its principles in our nonmonogamous relationships.

Defining Nonmonogamy

Broadly defined, nonmonogamy describes all consensual relationship structures that are, well ... not monogamous (romantic and sexual exclusivity with one partner at a time).

Somehow this is simultaneously really simple and really complex, and I notice folks tripping up on the language quite frequently. Even in choosing how to describe nonmonogamy, disagreements pop up within our communities. Should we call it consensual nonmonogamy, ethical nonmonogamy or just plain nonmonogamy? I'll rein in the neuro-dynamic urge to elaborate on everything, but this is an interesting and expansive discussion. In this text I will continue using "nonmonogamy," but please know that it's been quite a contemplative journey over the years to make this decision. Also, no shade to anyone who might have a different preference. We're all on our own journeys and as long as no one is intentionally causing anyone else harm, it's all good. I'm not here to "yuck any yums."

As someone who's been practising nonmonogamy since 2005, I have seen *so much* change in the language we use to describe it. I am still partnered with the superbabe who joined me in jumping ship from monogamy when we were shit-disturbing teenagers in love and back in our day, we didn't have Facebook and Reddit groups, libraries of books, or social media playlists engaging in public discourse about best practices in nonmonogamy. The way we once described our relationships wouldn't be appropriate or accurate for today's definitions.

We used to use the terms "polyamory" and "open relationship" interchangeably, and the now-controversial language of hierarchy[4] (words such as "primary" and "secondary") was pretty much the only option anyone was talking about. For a few years in my early 20s I would say that I had two primary partners. Now, I am like...what?

Even as I'm writing, the culture and language of nonmonogamy is evolving. I think this is both gorgeous and also potentially confusing for those of us who are seeking solid ground as we traverse new territory. So once more, while we're discussing the terms as they exist right now, some community members might choose to define and describe nonmonogamy differently.

As an analogy, think of the way the word "sports" is an umbrella term under which we find things like badminton, gymnastics and synchronized swimming. Now imagine if someone were to say "figure skating" when trying to describe sports, or use the words "swimming" and "sports" interchangeably. This would be super confusing and wildly inaccurate. It would also be hard to fully understand what they were talking about and would likely lead to misunderstanding and misinformation.

Unfortunately, this happens pretty often when discussing nonmonogamy. It's an umbrella or categorical term that covers many different types of relationships that fall outside of monogamy, and each one can be very different from the next.

Some of the relationship structures that fall under the nonmonogamy umbrella include:

- relationship anarchy
- swinging
- open relationships and marriages
- monogamish
- polyamory

This list is far from exhaustive, and I won't spend too much time defining the different types of nonmonogamous relationships. I think it's worth noting that some of them can overlap, some can be combined and some seem similar but actually look different in practice (just to keep us on our toes). Once you factor in the numerous subcategories for different relationship structures that also exist, it can become a lot to take in. I just want to highlight the expansiveness and diversity of relationships that fall under the nonmonogamy umbrella.

OK, but We Can't Not Talk Polyamory

I think I would be doing us all a disservice if I didn't talk about polyamory for a second. After all, babe is having a moment in the limelight! The more polyamory gets discussed in popular culture, the more it is subjected to monogamous values, ideals and expectations (Spoiler: We're already discussing the impact of mononormativity, but one thing at a time!). Today, there are TV shows referencing polyamory, many popular news outlets have released articles about it, and I've seen the term misused and misrepresented in ways that often cause more confusion, if not harm. (It's giving "swimming" when they mean to say "sports.")

Polyamory is one type of non-monogamy in which participants engage in multiple intimate, meaningful and loving relationships at once. The word "polyamory" breaks down into two words (in different root languages, much to some people's annoyance). *Poly*, which has Greek roots, means "many" as in "polygon," which is a shape with many sides. *Amory*, which has Latin roots, means "love" as in *amour* in French or *amore* in Italian. So, polyamory refers to relationships in which we have many loves.

Some subcategories and ways of practising polyamory include, but are not limited to:

- open or closed polyamory
- kitchen table, parallel or garden party polyamory
- hierarchical or non-hierarchical polyamory
- solo polyamory
- triads, quads and other groups of people engaged in relationships together

The function of sharing this is not to confuse you with terminology, or even to dig into the definitions. I am mostly trying to highlight how nuanced and diverse even *one* of the types of nonmonogamy can be, and how problematic it can be to lump them all into the same category. Between biased misconceptions and misleading media representation, polyamory is frequently used interchangeably with nonmonogamy and other nonmonogamous relationship structures.

I have a vivid memory from my early days of polyamory. At the time I was in my late teens, and in my circle of friends and acquaintances, superbabe partner and I were the only ones engaged in *consensual* nonmonogamy. Make no mistake, cheating was a very common expression of *non-consensual* nonmonogamy in our midst. In fact, being cheated on in monogamy is what made me realize that having multiple partners could make sense for me (but being deceived and lied to most certainly did not). I sort of became the go-to person when people had questions about nonmonogamy thanks to my "unusual" relationship.

The memory is of standing at a bus stop with a loose acquaintance who was kind of grilling me about the ins and outs of how we "supposedly" made it work. After I did a bunch of clarifying and explaining, they finally exclaimed, "Oh, I get it now! You get to date with none of the commitment!" I just sighed, probably rolled my eyes and said, "No. I'm more committed to this relationship than I have ever been before." Isn't it interesting that through the monogamous lens, this person somehow heard me describe my loving partnerships and still interpreted it as some version of playing the field?

Polyamory is not about sex. Yes, it is possible that people include sex with different partners in their practice of polyamory, but sex is not the focal point of this type of nonmonogamy. In fact, many people who practise this relationship style identify along the spectrum of asexuality (also known as "Ace" or the "Ace spectrum" and including many different identities that fall outside of allosexual or normative expressions of sexual attraction). Other types of nonmonogamy that are more focused on sex also exist—like swinging, for example. However, misusing the term "polyamory" when we're talking about orgies and sex parties can create incorrect associations and stereotypes while also marginalizing some community members.

Counter to these stereotypes, I was first exposed to the concept of asexuality through polyamory. Early on in my journey, one of my partners identified as asexual, a term I had never heard before. Partnering with this person opened my eyes to new types of human difference in a relationship that certainly did not revolve around sex. As I was a fairly horny teenager, it also taught me many lessons about my own sexuality as I worked tirelessly to deconstruct the social programming (also known as "unlearning a paradigm") that led me to correlate my worthiness with my sexual desirability. This work required immense self-reflection, super challenging conversations and negotiations, and—as I'm being totally honest—copious amounts of cannabis. The transformative potential of polyamorous relating taught me that it was *definitely* not about having sex.

We also hear the language of polyamory being used when people are seeking to have a sexual experience like a threesome, which is not the same thing. People who are polyamorous may engage in a threesome, but just because three people choose to have sex together does not mean that they are interested in building ongoing intimate and loving relationships together as well.

What's a Paradigm?

A paradigm is a perspective or way of seeing the world. It's our own internal operating system.

However, when most of society operates on a given paradigm, it creates a sort of social standard or norm for how we live our lives and expect others to live theirs.

In Marla-terms: A social paradigm is like the tea we're steeped in. No one questions why it smells like peppermint. Life's just peppermint, babes! And if peppermint is all we've ever known, we may never need to confront the reality that there might be cultures or communities swimming in ginger or nettle or whatever! That's the thing about widespread paradigms: No matter how strongly they smell or taste, we're so used to them that we don't even realize they exist.

When a paradigm is elevated to a social norm, it dictates the things a society adopts as the status quo. It's just what is.

It's important to note that paradigms can differ between places, cultures, languages, generations and beyond. Some are more widespread than others based on what a culture values. This is tricky, because we know that not everyone within any given culture will have the same values. We could get into the nitty-gritty of power dynamics in social systems and who has the authority to dictate social norms, but again, I'm going to do my best to rein in the urge to talk about all the things and keep us focused.

> **It is typical for defiant people to experience pushback from those privileged by the pre-existing social paradigm**

Let's take a low-hanging fruit example. Consider the social paradigm of capitalism and think of how our society treats those who are unemployed. Rather than questioning the functionality of capitalism, society instead promotes widespread stereotypes about laziness, drug involvement and alcoholism. Unemployed people are dehumanized and objectified as an expense to taxpayers. They are seen as a problem to be solved. People who defy social norms are often seen in a negative light by those who are benefiting from the status quo. Whether they are considered a threat, a burden or a problem, it is typical for those defiant people to experience pushback from those privileged by the pre-existing social paradigm, especially from those in positions of power.

What's interesting is that when a movement away from a social paradigm reaches a certain critical mass, we often see how people who are still entrenched in the status quo appropriate the language and ideas from new "fringe" or "radical" communities, while still actually working to uphold the old systems. Think of cryptocurrency. It is often presented as something groundbreaking and almost revolutionary, but in reality it's still connected to ideas of getting rich and gaining capital.

By practising nonmonogamy, we defy the foundations of the monogamous paradigm—in ourselves and in society. In a world that presents monogamy as the only style of relationship that is normal, natural, ethical or acceptable, nonmonogamous people become vulnerable to being stereotyped and discriminated against by systems and people in power and others who benefit from the status quo.

Mononormativity: Let's Dig In

Monogamy is just one type of relationship structure. People who choose this dynamic can practise it in healthy ways with care, open communication and trust. It can also be practised in harmful ways—monogamous people might cheat, act possessively or mistreat one another. But these behaviours are not exclusive to monogamy. *Any relationship structure can be practised in healthy or harmful ways.*

The thing is, monogamy has become embedded in the fabric of our society. Being part of a monogamous couple comes with benefits and privileges that are not accessible to people who are single or partnered with more than one person. For example, monogamy is encoded in legal systems. We can only marry one person, and there are benefits for those who choose to be married. From being entitled to make choices for loved ones if they are hospitalized to receiving non-taxable transfers of wealth if a spouse passes away, being in a legally binding monogamous union comes with incentives! In most countries it is not legal to marry more than one person, so to gain the systemic privileges of marriage, one must either practise monogamy or feign monogamy to the government.

I am one of those people who has chosen to perform monogamy. On our fifteenth anniversary, the partner I've mentioned a few times and I got married. I'll never forget the day I called my insurance company and it came up that I had gotten married since the last time I called. The kind person on the phone was so excited to share that I was now eligible for a $200 annual discount on my car insurance.

I was incensed and asked a series of probing questions (kindly! I've worked many years in the service industry) while highlighting the absurd inequity of rewarding people for having access to partnership and the privilege of getting married. The frazzled person at the call centre did some digging, spoke to a supervisor and ultimately chalked it up to statistics indicating that people who are married are less likely to be in car accidents (WTF?). Now, let's be real. You know that I took the discount—because capitalism—but I certainly let them know how fucked up that policy was.

All this to say that society operates within a deeply entrenched social paradigm of monogamy, which we can call mononormativity. In mononormativity, monogamy is portrayed as the normal and natural way to be in partnership. It is presented as the right and ethical way despite statistics around cheating indicating that it's far from foolproof.[5]

And from the macro level, it seeps into privileges, beliefs and interactions at the interpersonal micro level. Mononormativity presents itself in all kinds of subtle ways that we have come to expect as part of the status quo.

Here are some examples:

- "Are you bringing a plus-one to the event?"

- Love triangles on TV and in movies, where someone has to choose between multiple love interests.

- Legal and medical forms with room for only one emergency contact or next of kin.

A neurologist once asked me, "What is the gender of your partner?" I asked, "Which one?"

* CRICKETS *

This was likely a well-meaning attempt at inclusivity, even though it felt like they were taking a back-alley route to assess my sexual orientation, which had nothing to do with my brain scans. But even if I were practising monogamy, my response would not have accurately answered that question.

Nothing like a mononormativity combo with bisexual erasure!

The list of examples goes on, but the point here is that monogamy is a deeply entrenched social paradigm that is often unnoticed because it is "just how it is."

Is It Even Mononormativity Without Couple's Privilege?

Couple's privilege is the jelly to the peanut butter of mononormativity. Since The Monogamous Couple is at the core of the paradigm's existence, it sort of makes sense that they would be centred and rewarded for their participation. I'm not suggesting that when people have couple's privilege, we should hold it against them, but rather that we should be aware of it so that we can start thinking about how to dismantle it when it might be causing harm. This harm is not exclusive to nonmonogamous dynamics, but it shows up there quite frequently (more about this in part 3).

Let's start by getting clear about privilege. When I think of privilege, I think of a kind of access, power, status or advantage that is granted to specific individuals or groups as a by-product of their position in society. People are often unaware of their privilege. Some individuals are conscious of their privilege and work to use it for good or at least watch for its potential to do harm, while others take full advantage of it with or without regard for others. (Think back to the not-so-heroic moment when I accepted the discount on my car insurance. I was *very* clear about my privilege and chose to take advantage of it. Perhaps I had some regard for others, but I doubt that my strongly worded feedback had much impact on the system.) People who are not conscious of their privilege can be ignorant of the ways they might participate in the oppression and marginalization of others. The all-encompassing nature of some social paradigms can make it easy to take our privileges for granted, because again, it's "just how it is." It can also make it easy for even those with the best of intentions to cause harm.

Every broad social paradigm favours certain groups of people, creating a hierarchy of privilege and oppression in society. In mononormativity, monogamous couples are given the most status and power. This is couple's privilege.

As I mentioned earlier, couple's privilege is embedded in our legal systems and cultural norms. In addition to marriage, consider how much more affordable and accessible it is for couples to rent or purchase a home. Contemporary Western housing markets strongly favour dual incomes. I know many couples who share studio or bachelor apartments as a survival strategy in an increasingly unaffordable rental landscape. Yes, people have roommates, but finding them can be challenging and precarious for many reasons, and in most cases, it is more expensive to live with a roommate than a partner that you share a bed and groceries with. Plus, sharing a place with a roommate does not hold the same social meaning as moving in with a partner.

Within the context of nonmonogamy, certain kinds of privilege favour those who are in a core couple versus those who are dating on their own. For those who have children, couple's privilege can look like being able to lean on our parenting partner when we have a date night with someone else. People who parent solo may have to do a great deal of unseen labour to go on a date, such as soliciting and paying for childcare. Another common expression of couple's privilege in nonmonogamy happens when the people in the core or foundational couple prioritize their own feelings over those of other partners. This can leave external partners feeling disregarded, left out or objectified. Within this context, the person feeling marginalized by the couple's privilege might be very aware of its impact, while those in the position of privilege may be oblivious to it.

Mononormativity Can Cause Harm

Mononormativity can cause harm in different ways, and I'd like to spotlight two of them. The first is judgment and the second is misrepresentation and misappropriation.

1. JUDGMENT

If we come back to monogamy being portrayed as the right, normal, natural and ethical way to engage in intimate partnership, we don't have to stretch our imaginations too far to see how society would categorize anything else as wrong, abnormal, unnatural and unethical. If this is how society frames nonmonogamy, how are the people who engage in alternative relationships perceived? Unfortunately, they are othered, judged, villainized and pathologized.

As nonmonogamy becomes more widespread, quite expectedly, more backlash emerges from those who are clinging to the paradigm of mononormativity. I don't necessarily blame them. People tend to be threatened by things they don't understand, and media portrayals of contemporary nonmonogamy have only fanned the flames of bias and misinformation. Keep in mind that our society privileges monogamy and condemns anything else, so individuals who are raised in these systems are indoctrinated to see nonmonogamy in a negative light.

Similar to outliers in the paradigm of capitalism, in the context of mononormativity we find all kinds of biased and disparaging stereotypes about people who engage in nonmonogamy presented as truth. Here are some common examples of harmful mononormative ideas about nonmonogamy:

- If a nonmonogamous relationship fails, nonmonogamy is to blame.

- "It's just sanctioned cheating!"
- It's all about having lots of sex and orgies.
- It's the same thing as being single.
- Everyone has sexually transmitted infections.

These kinds of stereotypes can be presented as humorous in some circumstances, and quite biting and accusatory in others. It is one thing for monogamy to be a statistical norm—what most people do most of the time. However, when we judge others—or ourselves—based on our own perception of what is normal, there can be harmful repercussions. People have shared stories with me about being ostracized by friends, family and community after sharing that they're nonmonogamous. One person told me that a friend stopped speaking to them out of fear that they would hit on this friend's partner—as though being nonmonogamous makes us attracted to everyone, and makes us completely throw away any prior sense of morals or boundaries.

Historically, the news, films and TV shows have portrayed polygamy (marriage to multiple partners) as a "barbaric" form of nonmonogamy. Emphasizing coercive fringe religious cults or faraway "primitive" cultures whose practices Westerners see as "uncivilized," mononormativity has long regarded nonmonogamous relationships and people as anything from inferior to monstrous.

Which people and cultures have been called those words, and by whom? Please consider who has historically held power over the narratives that are shared or silenced by popular media. We cannot ignore that mononormativity exists in disturbing harmony with other oppressive systems and paradigms (such as white supremacy[6] and misogyny,[7] to name two). We cannot investigate social paradigms without noticing interconnected systems of power and how the privileged few use their social power over those who have less.

In my work as a relationship therapist specializing in non-monogamy, I've heard stories of therapists who have suggested that nonmonogamy is the reason for all of someone's mental health challenges. I've also heard of therapists ending working relationships with nonmonogamous people because they judged their clients' relationships to be unethical or viewed those relationships as a form of cheating. I have found myself supporting people who were not only struggling with whatever challenges they were already working through, but also the trauma of being discriminated against by supposed helping professionals.

All this to say that some social paradigms are insidious in the way they create hierarchies of privilege and power, and therefore those who fall out of line are likely to find themselves in positions of oppression and marginalization. While nonmonogamy is definitely becoming more commonplace, nonmonogamous people still have a long way to go in terms of having equal rights and privileges in society.

2. MISREPRESENTATION AND MISAPPROPRIATION

Certain kinds of nonmonogamy have taken centre stage in pop culture and media. As mentioned, polyamory has been having a moment in the spotlight and this has both advantages and disadvantages. On the one hand, simply portraying multiple options for relationship structures is a step in the direction of challenging mononormative narratives. On the other hand, how is nonmonogamy being portrayed, and by whom?

Nonmonogamy is often depicted as a lifestyle rather than a relationship orientation. If we see nonmonogamy as a lifestyle, it's easy to assume it to be a fad or something we can take or leave. Now, keep in mind that some people are comfortable participating in different relationship structures at different times in their lives. The term for this is "ambiamorous." These people may choose polyamory (and perhaps other types of nonmonogamy) in certain partnerships and feel just as content in monogamy for others.

However, for many like me, nonmonogamy is a relationship orientation and part of identity. If I were only involved with one partner, I would still maintain the freedom to engage in multiple sexy, consenting, intimate, loving partnerships. Even if I were single, I would still be nonmonogamous. Portraying nonmonogamy as a lifestyle or a fleeting phase ignores those of us who are not only deeply committed to our partners, but also to these ways of relating.

Pop-cultural portrayals of nonmonogamy also typically include the prevalence of whiteness, gender conformity, unrealistic beauty standards, affluence, heterosexuality (unless it includes bisexual cisgender[8] women, because they are more socially accepted, and are often depicted as "good times" for cisgender men) and, of course, the glorification of sex.

In reality, people from all walks of life practise nonmonogamy and many of them defy the limited mainstream representations. Often, people engaged in nonmonogamy occupy other positions of marginalization and oppression within society. For example, many are people of global majority (not white), 2SLGBTQIA+ folks, disabled people and so many others. Unfortunately, they become invisible when the media exoticizes nonmonogamy as a sexy thing that "hot" couples can try for a little while to "spice things up." And if it's not fun, they can just shut it down, right?

The danger of normalizing inaccurate media representations of nonmonogamous people and relationships is that it models nonmonogamy through a mononormative lens. The idea that couples can "try it out" without consequence is absolutely false. I'd also like to highlight the fact that nonmonogamy is being portrayed with couples at the core of the experience. Suddenly this is sounding a lot like monog... Think back to our earlier discussion of paradigms and capitalism. When ideas that negate the norms and values of a paradigm reach a critical mass, those in power will try to hold on to the original paradigm while pretending to be "alternative," "adventurous" thought leaders who break the mould. Like wow, crypto is absolutely *nothing* like capitalism—it's just designed and owned by gazillionaires who increase their capital through a new avenue. *Groundbreaking!*

In the Western context, nonmonogamy has gained enough popularity for those invested in mononormativity to take notice and take action. People with privilege, power and reach (journalists, film and TV producers, social media influencers) have commandeered the narrative away from the communities who have actively been engaged in nonmonogamy for centuries. Now, it is being packaged in the mainstream as a luxury experience for cisgender straight couples, which does not take into consideration the feelings, needs or experiences of outsiders who might be interested in dating these cisgender straight couples.

We see the concept of the throuple being touted as a couple bringing a third into their relationship and it all being breezy. Now don't get me wrong, throuples and triads—when three people are engaged in a polyamorous relationship together—are very real and this relationship structure can be rewarding, consenting and healthy for all involved. However, if the setup of that triad looks like a preexisting couple bringing a third person into their lives, often the couple will have the power to set the tone and pace of the relationship, leaving the third person marginalized in the dynamic. If it doesn't work out, the couple can blame nonmonogamy for the failure without investigating the ways that they may not have had the tools or resources to effectively manage relationships while learning a completely new way of relating.

This is the mononormative paradigm continuing to grip onto power as people begin to consider different relationship structures. I recognize that nonmonogamous relationships are still very much a minority in most of the world, but it seems that more people are seeing monogamy's shortcomings and seeking alternatives. Unfortunately, without the proper support, reflection, preparation and scaffolding, people trying to enter the completely new paradigm of nonmonogamous relating will tend to carry over the norms, values and expectations they have always known from monogamy, which can be quite a challenging set-up.

Part II Concepts in Action

Congratulations! You've made it to the part where we can start reflecting on the process of deconstructing mononormativity.

Remember, we're talking about unlearning a paradigm, and that's not "chill." By investigating the impact of mononormativity in our lives, we are taking a step away from our security blanket. It can be exciting and inspire growth, but it can also be destabilizing at times. Reshaping how we think about relationships can take some getting used to, but we've got this!

The Trap of Toxic Positivity

Toxic positivity is the phenomenon that occurs when we only pay attention to the positive or happy feelings while minimizing or ignoring hardships or struggles. Through the lens of toxic positivity, it's easy to abandon important feelings or parts of ourselves by explaining them away, pretending they don't exist, or even shaming ourselves for experiencing them at all. My ears always perk up like a cat when I hear people say that they're "not supposed" to feel a certain way.

The first time I experienced this phenomenon was in 2004, before I had embarked on my own nonmonogamy adventure. I was 17 and my best friend at the time was in a class with a prof who essentially ran a chaotic ethics non-class where he would show up, drop a contentious subject and sit back while a room full of riled-up teenagers engaged in heated debate for an hour and a half. This professor, who was at the edge of retirement, happened to be in a polyamorous marriage, and he would explain the ins and outs of his family dynamics to his classes. (You bet I audited his class the next semester for fun—all the debate, none of the assignments!)

My bestie emerged from this class completely sold on the topic of polyamory. To be clear, she was not someone who was easily swayed. I would describe her as having a resting critical face. But she was genuinely challenged and impressed by the professor, who made so many valid arguments in favour of the ethics and morals of nonmonogamy. She was all in! She would rant about monogamy's dominance and control over others, ask why we have a limit on how much we can love, and question why it is acceptable to enjoy intimate friendships with others, but not to share sexuality. I agreed with the points she was making, and I live by many of them now, but damn, she was so full on about it.

It almost felt like she was trying to convince me that nonmonogamy was somehow the best kind of relationship—which to this day, I do not agree with. I'm here for *healthy* relationships, no matter what structure they take. I remember telling her that I got it *and* that I just wasn't interested in seeing anyone other than the one person I was dating at the time.

With all the burning passion and love in her heart, my dear friend went on to twist and misuse the fundamental tenets of polyamory to justify cheating on her monogamous partner. Breaking boundaries and deceiving our partners is not an effective way to practise non-monogamy (or any kind of relationship), but if all we've known is monogamy, it can be really hard to imagine even broaching the subject of nonmonogamy with loved ones, never mind acting on it.

When we idealize a concept, it becomes easy to ignore potential flaws in its design, and if we cease to think critically, we can become rigid or dogmatic in the way we view it. As we learn about the values and the ethics of nonmonogamy, it is easy to put it on a pedestal.

Philosophically, the concept makes a lot of sense. We can become almost intoxicated by the *idea* of nonmonogamy, but that doesn't necessarily prepare us for the whiplash that can arise when mononormativity creeps in as we try to put nonmonogamy into practice.

If you ever catch yourself or loved ones in a state of toxic positivity about nonmonogamy, it might be helpful to peek below the surface to make sure that no one is dismissing the possibility of the real challenges that can arise as well. Also, just because things have been "good vibes only" so far, doesn't mean that can't change. I'd love to make promises that if we work diligently enough, all our relationships (nonmonogamous or otherwise) will become easy and carefree. But I'd be lying, and that's not really my brand.

Of course, we can also experience pure ecstasy and magic in our nonmonogamous dynamics! If it was all a gruelling slog, I wouldn't still be here investing so much into my nonmonogamous world. I often joke that no one hires me for my poker face. I want to be authentic and real with you about the tough stuff *and* the incredible stuff. All to say, beware falling into the trap of idealizing nonmonogamy.

Here are examples of toxic positivity to watch out for as you explore nonmonogamy:

- "We never get jealous" or "I'm not a jealous person."
  - Jealousy is a complex emotional experience that anyone can have. Some of us might experience it more or differently than others, but no one is impervious to jealousy.

- The glorification and expectation of compersion.
    - » Compersion is the feeling of joy and excitement we have for our partners as they experience success and love with their other partners. Compersion is a wonderful feeling, but it is not a fair expectation to set for ourselves. Some of us may struggle to ever access compersion and we can still be in rewarding, healthy nonmonogamous relationships.

- "Everyone gets along."
    - » Do they? Maybe that's true right now, but this is a dangerous expectation to set when multiple relationships and personalities are in the mix.

> "Nonmonogamous relationships are more evolved." No. They're not.

- “Nonmonogamous relationships are more evolved.”
    - » No. They’re not. This can be a dangerous belief and lead to some real high-horse judgy stuff.

- “Everyone is treated equally.”
    - » While we might strive for equity in our relationships, equality is rarely possible, or even desirable, because we all have different needs and wants.

Practising Takes Practice

Imagine that you are a fierce tennis player (sure, let’s “sports” again). You’ve been playing since you were young and you’ve played against many opponents. You understand the rules and have become so comfortable with the racquet that it almost feels like an extension of your arm. One day you discover football and something about it is calling to you, so you decide to give it a try. You read the rulebooks, watch football on TV and consult some friends who know the game well.

Do you expect that you are going to be a stellar football player the first time you get on the field? Would you think it reasonable to get angry with yourself every time you fumble? Maybe those among us with perfectionistic tendencies are smirking right now! In reality, no matter how much tennis practice you have under your belt, you'll likely anticipate that it's going to take time to learn how to play football—even if you wish you were a superstar from the start.

I've noticed that people who are starting to practise nonmonogamy—a completely unfamiliar relationship structure—frequently do not offer themselves the grace and space to be learners. Almost like because they've been in relationships before, they afford themselves less or no space for making the inevitable mistakes that come with trying anything for the first time. From where I'm sitting, it feels pretty unfair and unkind to put pressure on ourselves, and sometimes each other, to get it right from the start. It's giving tennis pro expecting to be a football superstar without any practice.

You can read every book you can find about nonmonogamy, listen to all the podcasts and follow all the educators on social media, but I'm going to be real with you: We can only get so far by reading theory. Until we are in situations where we are actually feeling the feelings or having the trauma responses, it's hard to know how we're going to react or put the theory into practice.

To be clear, I am most certainly not nay-saying preparedness! The importance of putting in the proactive labour of learning about nonmonogamy before jumping in is invaluable, and I cannot stress that enough. I have been doing this work personally and professionally for long enough to know that "humaning" is not an exact science, and mistakes happen. I'm not just talking to those who are brand-new to nonmonogamy—I've been practising nonmonogamy full on for many years and it's literally my job, and I still fuck up!

Thirteen years into our nonmonogamous relationship, one of my partners and I moved in together. Not too long after that, we connected with someone new and the two of them fell really hard and fast in love. I was slowly developing my own relationship with this new person, but it was different, and certainly more complicated and tentative. I found myself experiencing all kinds of feelings in ways that I had never felt before: jealousy, resentment, anger, fear, unworthiness, loneliness and so much more.

At the time, I had been a non-monogamy educator for years, and was training to become a therapist. I remember telling myself things like, "This is your job—you can't feel this way" and "You consented and signed up for this kind of relationship, so you can't be mad at them." I was dismissing and invalidating my real feelings under the guise that I was somehow above or beyond them. Toxic positivity, anyone? *Who was I kidding?* I was not then, nor am I now, above or beyond being human! It took me heaps of therapy, introspection and incredibly challenging conversations with both of the individuals involved to realize that my feelings were valid. Upon deeper reflection, I was able to investigate the feelings to understand where they were coming from, what I could learn from them and what changes were needed to better support everyone involved.

I'm sharing this story because it's an example of how important it is to remember that at any point along the way, we can still make mistakes or feel really painful feelings. No amount of preparation or training can protect us from struggling sometimes. Holding ourselves to unreachable standards of perfection will only constipate us as we work through the tough stuff. We can move through our challenges so much more smoothly if we give ourselves permission to be imperfect human beings.

I don't think that practice makes perfect. I think practice leads to more experiences and opportunities to make mistakes, and hopefully learn and grow from them. Aiming for perfection is almost certainly a set-up for inglorious failure.

I'm also not suggesting that we aim to cause harm or shirk accountability for our actions—quite the opposite! Making mistakes in relationships can often result in getting hurt or hurting people we care about. If we invest in ourselves and our relationships by learning skills and tools for developing self-awareness, healthy communication and boundaries, we can learn to repair from rupture as a way to build intimacy and closeness in relationships. If this sounds scary, that makes sense. Engaging in relationships is risky business and even though you can get hurt, if you've read this far, you're probably one of the brave souls who has decided that the risk is worth it, even if it takes a lot of hard work and practice.

Hard doesn't equal bad. It's just hard.

Unlearning a Paradigm: Let's Be Kind to Ourselves

Unlearning a paradigm takes patience and perseverance. I often liken it to the process of a child trying to remove a snowsuit in winter. Let me explain.

Imagine a kid, maybe four or five years old. It's a crisp winter day and heaps of snow cover the ground. They're stoked to play in it! If they had a tail, it would be wagging. Their loving guardian now takes on the seemingly endless task of getting them geared up to go outside. They put on a hat, a scarf, snow pants, a jacket, one mitten, then the next. Kiddo can barely contain their excitement! They're ready to run out the door but they still need to put on their boots. They are so bundled up that they look like a penguin who can barely bring their arms down to their sides from all the layering.

The guardian throws on their own winter gear as quickly as possible while kiddo is on the verge of a meltdown because they're now overheating and waiting two minutes feels like two hours. Finally, the door swings open and our tiny human gleefully faceplants into the closest snowbank. Our exasperated guardian steps outside, closes the door, turns around, and standing at their feet is the cutest little snow angel exclaiming, "I have to pee!"

If you know, you know.

It would be convenient if our noble guardian could snap their fingers and kiddo would be undressed and ready for potty time. But alas, this is not Clark Kent hopping into a phone booth and emerging moments later as Superman. So begins the laborious and highly time-sensitive task of removing the layers. One boot, then the next, one mitten, then the next... Kiddo is wiggling around, whimpering that they can't hold it for much longer.

I could go on, but I'm going to stop here and say that it is beyond likely that this kid is not going to make it to the bathroom before they have an accident in their snowsuit.

Unlearning a paradigm is a lot like our little buddy trying to make it to the bathroom in time. So many bulky layers of thoughts, beliefs, values, judgments, misconceptions and expectations need to be shed, which takes investment, time and patience.

No matter how much work we've put in, it seems like some sneaky remnant from whatever paradigm we've been trying to deconstruct is always waiting to surprise us when we least expect it. I hate to be the bearer of bad news, but sometimes we're not going to make it to the proverbial potty in time, no matter how hard we try. Sometimes, we're going to piss the snowsuit.

Let's remember that paradigms are integrated in everything we know to be real. Their values are reflected in the fabric of society, from politics to family gatherings to our favourite songs and TV shows. If we are going to try to deconstruct or go as far as *unlearning* a paradigm, we might want to prepare ourselves for the likelihood that things will not go as planned.

Personally, I'd rather be prepared to piss the snowsuit than be taken by surprise. As mentioned earlier, backlash and fallout can come from those who are entrenched in the paradigm, and we're also confronted with internal challenges as we work to shift perspectives away from that which we've always known. I'm not sharing this to scare or deter you, but rather to invite you to be kind to yourself through this magnificent process.

If we remember that we are taking on the brave task of challenging the status quo, knowing that perfection is not the goal and that we will sometimes falter, we can also take steps toward preparing to be gentle with ourselves and our loved ones when it happens.

PERSONAL REFLECTION: SELF-COMPASSION

I know that self-compassion may not come easily to many of us. Here are some reflection questions to ignite the process of developing compassion toward yourself. They can be used as introspective tools and as conversation prompts to use with loved ones of all kinds.

- How can I be accountable when I've made mistakes or unintentionally caused harm, without judging or shaming myself?
- How can I disentangle my behaviour from my identity?
    - How can I think of my mistake as a thing I did instead of who I am (for example, a "bad person")?

- What kind of language do I use to speak to myself in my mind? Do I call myself mean names? Do I use a critical tone?
    - » If I discover critical language within, what are some examples of gentler language I could use to replace harsh words?

- How do I typically express disappointment in myself?
    - » What kind of strategy might help me to express it more effectively (for example, pausing a conversation until later, going for a walk, speaking with a trusted loved one)?

Conflict Is Not a Four-Letter Word

Part of preparing ourselves for the process of deconstructing mononormativity can involve bolstering our communication skills for the moments when conflict arises. Even the idea of conflict can have some of us ducking for cover. If we have only ever known conflict to look like big fights or feeling shame or rejection, then of course it would feel like a four-letter word to be avoided at all costs.

The reality is that conflict happens in little ways all the time, such as trying to do something as simple as choosing a movie to watch. Holding others accountable for their actions while simultaneously showing care and compassion can take practice, but it's just as important as learning to do this for ourselves. If we are prepared for the inevitability that we will run into relational hiccups, then we can bolster ourselves proactively with tools to work through challenging moments together.

Let's imagine that you are seeing someone new and you're getting ready for a date night. You have another partner who is aware that you're going on this date, and consents to the nonmonogamous dynamic, but as the afternoon approaches, they are struggling with insecurity. Maybe they call you and share how they're feeling. Maybe a few hours before your date they ask if they can come over to chat. Maybe they share that they feel really uncomfortable about you going on this date or that they wish you wouldn't go at all.

How might you respond? Do you choose to postpone or cancel the date? Do you decide to check in with this partner while you're out on the date? Do you tell this person that they're out of line for behaving this way, or that they're asking for something unreasonable? None of these options are right or wrong and there are many more ways someone could respond. I just want to point out that sometimes we may be confronted by other people's challenges and processes in ways that conflict with our own needs and desires.

I can imagine being frustrated with someone if we made previous agreements and at the last minute they seem to change their mind. Even having to do unexpected emotional labour while trying to get ready to go on a date can be overwhelming. However, if I care for someone and they're struggling, I would want to support them. Do you see how the line between showing up for the needs of others while also showing up for our own needs can become blurred?

It's beneficial to think about how we engage when we're feeling challenged, affronted or frustrated. We all have different communication styles and tendencies, which are often rooted in things like our cultures, families of origin, past relational wounds and traumas, and attachment styles.[9] Some of us might be more confrontational and others more conflict avoidant. We might also behave differently with one partner compared to another, or compared to a family member.

Developing awareness of our own communication styles and tendencies can help us to see the patterns of things that might ignite us to become defensive, avoidant, overwhelmed, frustrated, judgmental or shut down. From there, it can allow us to be more attuned and sensitized to our patterns of communication with others so that we can collaborate in strategizing how to have the most effective conversations possible, even when things are challenging.

My personal bias is thinking that more healthy communication is better. From both my personal and professional experience, I have noticed that if we work toward kind, compassionate, accountable and assertive communication, it helps to pave the way toward healthy and rewarding relationships. If we can engage in conflict from the perspective that repair is possible, we can increase trust and intimacy in our relationships by reframing rupture as something that can lead to growth. Of course, yelling at someone or walking away from them in the middle of a conversation without warning is still technically communication and I am certainly not endorsing that!

Healthy communication can include things like checking for consent before launching into a challenging conversation, taking breaks if things are becoming heated or overwhelming or using text and voice messages as alternatives to face-to-face conversations. Coming up with strategies that work for us as well as our loved ones is an essential part of being able to navigate conflict effectively—no matter how big or small the issue.

A Note on Safety and Boundaries

Developing strategies for compassionate communication stops being the main priority when there is a lack of safety (physical, mental, emotional or spiritual). While I would not typically suggest exiting a conversation suddenly without warning, if you are ever feeling unsafe or attacked in communication with someone, this may be the healthiest response. Safety comes first!

Another thing to keep in mind is that sometimes being kind to others can look like disengaging or saying "no" respectfully. If we're dealing with someone who is judging or harassing us, it is absolutely valid—and part of healthy and compassionate communication—to set boundaries and follow through with them.

For example, if someone is asking invasive questions, it is entirely within your rights to say something like, "I am feeling uncomfortable discussing this topic, but I am happy to provide resources for you to learn the answers to your questions." If this does not end the nonconsensual discourse, you could follow up with something like, "As I said, I would rather not talk about this. If we can't move on to another topic of conversation, I will have to leave or hang up the call." You

have now named the boundary and if you were to follow through, it would be part of healthy communication.

PERSONAL REFLECTION: COMPASSIONATE COMMUNICATION

Here are some questions to support you in developing compassionate communication with others. I invite you to use these prompts as introspective tools or as conversation starters with loved ones to help collaborate on developing communication strategies together.

- How can I hold other people accountable for their mistakes, and possibly for causing harm, without judging them?
- What kind of language do I use toward others when I'm feeling angry or

hurt (out loud to them, behind their backs or even in my own head)?

   » Do I tend to attack or yell? Do I tend to get quiet or broody? Do I tend to judge easily or dismiss my own feelings? These are just a few possible examples.

- If I notice that I am being mean or critical in communication with others, what could be some alternative ways to express myself without judgment?

- What strategies can I use during times of conflict if I notice that tensions are rising or that I am overwhelmed? For example, asking to pause the conversation for a clear amount of time.

Part III When Mononormativity Shows Up Uninvited

Let's explore the ways that mononormativity can show up like an uninvited guest to our nonmonogamous dinner party.

In this section we'll look at some common themes and examples that I have either experienced personally or seen in my professional work. As much as we can grow from making our own mistakes, if we're lucky we can also learn from others who made mistakes before us, so that we don't have to.

In this section I offer reflection questions that are intended to be adapted for wherever you might be on your relationship journey. For example, if a question is framed in the context of someone who has not yet begun to practise nonmonogamy and you are already active in nonmonogamy, I encourage you to adjust the phrasing so that it makes sense in your own experience (and of course, keep what works and leave the rest).

How Do We Unpack Couple's Privilege?

I want to come back to couple's privilege because it's such an integral part of mononormativity that it's impossible to escape, even in nonmonogamy. Whether it shows up in committed polyamorous relationships or in casual sexy adventures, once two or more people are in the mix, couple's privilege is afoot. Please remember that I am not suggesting that couple's privilege is inherently bad or that prioritizing each other sometimes is a misuse of power. The idea is to acknowledge the existence of the power we hold as a couple so that we don't unintentionally use it to marginalize others.

The following questions can be used by couples to explore the impact of couple's privilege and as an opening to deconstructing the phenomenon. They can be helpful for individuals who might be getting involved with someone who's already in an established couple, or with both members of the couple, to explore on their own or with their partners. These questions are meant to initiate conversations and are by no means a complete picture of all the ways that couple's privilege can emerge as we practise nonmonogamy.

REFLECTIONS ON COUPLE'S PRIVILEGE

- How does couple's privilege express itself in our relationship?
- When dating individually, how can our couple's privilege impact our partners and metamours (my partner's other partners, who I am not dating)?

- When dating someone together, how can we make sure that their needs are prioritized as much as our own?

- When dating someone together, do we have expectations that we must both date this person? If one of us wants to break up with them, does the other have to break up with them as well?
  - » What if one of us connects more easily with a shared partner?

- How do our relationship boundaries and agreements impact other partnerships?
  - » Do we have expectations around holidays, sleepovers or vacations?
    - If so, how do they reinforce or dismantle couple's privilege?

- If one of us were struggling with nonmonogamy, or with our metamour, would closing our relationship or taking a break from nonmonogamy be an option?

  - If so, how could that impact our other partners?
  - What might be some strategies to consider the needs of other partners if one of us were struggling?

- Are we prepared to share with family and friends that we are practising nonmonogamy?
  - How could this impact new partners entering our dynamic?

- How could we maintain our individual and shared needs and boundaries with new partners while also making space to negotiate based on their needs and boundaries?

What If It Feels like Cheating?

Imagine you've done tons of work to learn about nonmonogamy and you're feeling ready to give it a shot. Whether you have a partner who you're opening up with or you are starting out on your own solo adventure, at some point you find yourself with one partner and then others come into your life.

This is the time to start putting all the learning and unlearning into practice. But what happens if you start seeing someone new and it feels like you're doing something wrong? Or what if your partner starts seeing someone new and it feels like they're cheating on you, even if you know from an intellectual perspective that they're not?

Please know that if you ever feel this way, you are not alone! If everything you've ever known about intimate partnerships has come through mononormativity, then you would have always believed it's right to invest exclusively in one monogamous relationship. That exclusivity has been the defining feature in making those relationships special, real and sacred. It makes sense for it to feel like the rug is being pulled out from underneath you as you try to convince yourself that "the truth" is actually false. The cognitive dissonance is real!

I've heard people describe their relationships as feeling less sacred or special if they're sharing themselves or their partners with other people. Mononormativity can leave us feeling devalued or like we are devaluing others when we break its rules. But no relationship or person is spoiled or tainted by engaging in multiple consenting relationships. It takes time to realize that every relationship has unique dynamics that makes it special or sacred, and these have nothing to do with how many people we explore partnership with.

It's also important to consider how sex-negativity can enter the chat when the idea of cheating arises. If you ever catch yourself or partners feeling disgusted or turned off after someone has been on a date with another person and no one broke any boundaries or relationship agreements, the issues might stem from social conditioning. Rather than villainizing or blaming one another, you could use this valuable moment for self-reflection and putting those communication skills to work. It can take a great deal of vulnerability to honestly name the cringy feelings that are coming up for us (like jealousy, insecurity, disgust or fear) without seeking to control or change another person.

What If My Partner Likes Someone More and Leaves Me?

This one is tough, and I've seen it come up time and time again. Part of what makes it so challenging is that this fear can absolutely become a reality. But it has nothing to do with nonmonogamy, even though mononormativity would have us believe otherwise.

Let's get into this by investigating monogamous relationship dynamics. Scenarios in which one partner falls for someone new and leaves their previous relationship happen all the time in monogamy. In some ways, this can actually be the best-case scenario because within the mononormative paradigm, the only other alternative is cheating. Please keep in mind that we can meet new people in places such as school, work, art classes, grocery stores and bars and that we do not need to be on dating apps in order to develop chemistry with someone new.

One completely normalized phenomenon in mononormativity is serial monogamy. It describes the practice of consistently jumping out or leaving one monogamous partnership for another with no time or space between relationships. By design, this style of monogamy requires meeting someone new and choosing them over a previous partner. If this is a common practice within mononormative culture, then of course that fear can transfer over to nonmonogamy. The freedom to explore multiple relationships is actually a set-up for being able to remain in multiple relationships at once, rather than having to trade one for another.

However, there's a prerequisite for experiencing healthy relationships with multiple partners: The relationships need to be healthy. (I'm saying "healthy" but we can also interchange that for "safe," "rewarding" or "fulfilling" in this scenario.) Unfortunately, sometimes people find themselves in relationships where things are not really functioning beneath the surface, and rather than working to improve the state of affairs or ending the dynamic amicably, they either continue as is or begin to explore nonmonogamy as a way of staying together and having their needs met elsewhere.

One of the founding principles of nonmonogamy is that we cannot expect any one person to meet all of our needs. In fact, we all meet different needs in various relationships, even if we are monogamous. However, if our *fundamental* needs are not being met in a partnership (and these needs can look different from person to person), chances are that resentment will build, along with other uncomfortable feelings lurking beneath the surface of the dynamic. We can easily dismiss our own dissatisfaction when fundamental needs are not being met under the influence of toxic positivity. It can tell us that dissatisfaction is normal, or that we shouldn't expect too much of our partner. Staying in a relationship that does not feel healthy is not what we mean when we say that we can't meet all our needs in one relationship.

Now imagine that some vital unmet needs are brewing beneath the surface of a relationship as we start seeing someone new. If we're hitting it off with a new partner, the first thing we have to contend with is new relationship energy (NRE).[10] In this period, everything about the person is shiny and exciting. NRE is literally intoxicating from a neurochemical perspective, and we can easily become hyper-fixated on this new person. (For me, the added dopamine deficiency from ADHD can make NRE feel addictive, and I have to work diligently to keep myself grounded and honest, so I don't burn out from chasing the "happy" neurochemicals.[11])

Through the lens of mononormativity we're taught to compare and rank our relationships, placing partners at the top of the hierarchy. If we are intoxicated by NRE and all the amazing feelings associated with this new person, mononormative thinking would have us comparing the different dynamics and we would be predisposed to think we have to choose one partner over the other. If we are fundamentally unwell or dissatisfied in our existing relationship, the choice almost makes itself.

Additionally, given that mononormativity has been our dominant framework for understanding relationships for most of our lives, if we find ourselves satisfied in one relationship while dissatisfied in another, would it not then make sense to fall back on the habits and patterns we've always known? Mononormativity has a quick-fix "solution" for this: serial monogamy!

So, what's the antidote to this problem? *More healthy communication.* If we are avoiding hard conversations or conflict in our relationships, it's so easy for resentment to grow beneath the surface. This is why we talked about conflict and the value of bolstering our self-awareness and communication styles and creating communication protocols and strategies in our relationships.

If you ever have a partner share concern that you will leave them for a new relationship, here are a few things to consider:

- Am I actually committed to staying in this relationship, or is my partner pointing to a reality that something is not working between us? How do I feel when they share this with me?

- Is this concern stemming from my partner's trauma or relationship history, or is there something in our relational dynamic that is contributing to these feelings? Could it be some of both?

- How can I be compassionate and honest with both of us?

- What can I do to reassure my partner and help them feel more secure?

- Is my partner experiencing insecurity because of something happening in our relationship, or are they struggling to "shed the skin" of mononormativity? How can we support one another in this process?

If you are the one having these feelings, you can also ask these questions of yourself as you consider how to communicate your concerns to your partner.

What If My Partner's Attraction to Someone Else Makes Them Less Attracted to Me?

Mononormativity is a paradigm of scarcity. It makes us believe in a finite amount of love, sex, care, intimacy and loyalty. So, if my partner or I share some of those "finite" resources, we must somehow be subtracting or taking them away from each other. Please remember that we've been programmed to believe this, and nothing is wrong with you or anyone else for expressing the values of our social norms.

Imagine that through the framework of mononormativity, we're each holding a cup filled with love, attraction or both. When we enter a monogamous partnership, we essentially offer our partner everything in the cup. If we were to meet a new person with whom we wanted to share love or attraction, it would mean that we'd have to divide the contents of our cup between people. By this logic, having love or attraction for multiple people necessitates giving everyone a little less.

What if I were to suggest that while that logic is sound, the premise is incorrect? What if I said there was more than one cup? Imagine now that I have infinite cups of love and attraction, and every time I choose to give one to someone, they get to have the entire contents of a cup that is just for them. In this paradigm shift, if I have love or attraction for one person, it has no bearing on any of those feelings that I have for anyone else. The cups may have different liquids inside, but they don't need to be compared. Each one is just as unique as our relationships. When I talk about this, I never pass up the opportunity to have an Oprah moment: "You get a cup, and you get a cup, and EVERYBODY GETS A CUP!"

Nonmonogamy teaches us that an abundance of love, sex, care, intimacy and loyalty exists (not to be confused with infinite time and energy, which is a *very* different negotiation), but in order

Nonmonogamy teaches us that an abundance of love, sex, care, intimacy and loyalty exists.

to really *know* this on a nervous system level, we often have to experience it several times. I encourage you to be patient in this process. You're essentially trying to train yourself to believe in something you've never imagined to be possible—it might take some getting used to.

Conclusion

Real talk: I want to say *so much more!* I have many thoughts about interrelated topics swirling around in my head, but as discussed, sometimes taking a pause is the best course of action. I know the amount of information in this little mini-babe of a book is a lot to digest.

Through definitions, metaphors, stories and self-reflections, I hope you can come back to this conversation to remind yourself of the hard work and dedication that is required to challenge the status quo. Maybe it can even serve as a reminder of how far you've already come. Thinking about deconstructing mononormativity is already so much to take in, but acting on it in a world that's soaked in its values takes time, patience and heaps of compassion!

Allow me to leave you with this gentle reminder: It's hard to stay dry in the rain and we are almost certainly going to piss the snowsuit. So, let's be kind to ourselves and others, friends. *We're defying a freaking paradigm!*

Notes

1 It's wild to me that I was educating others about nonmonogamy with such little lived experience, but back in 2009 the subject received much less attention than it does today. It was not as easy to find elders and veterans who were discussing these topics publicly. Keep in mind that social media was not as it is today.

2 Two-Spirit, lesbian, gay, bisexual, transgender, Queer, questioning, intersex, asexual, aromantic and beyond.

3 A polycule is a group or web of nonmonogamous people who share relationships, even though they may not all be dating. This can look like partners and metamours (people who share a partner, but are not dating one another).

4 Hierarchy is an incredibly loaded topic in nonmonogamy discourse. I would love to get into it more, but I could write a whole separate book on the topic. As much as I hate to gloss over it, I will simply acknowledge that people hold different—frequently opposing—perspectives on hierarchy. I recommend exploring the topic for yourself to get clear on what makes sense for you and your partners to engage in consenting relationships together.

5 Hannah Sparks, "Chivalrous Men Cheat as Much as Misogynists—and More Women Need to Know That: Study," New York Post, August 25, 2024, https://nypost.com/2024/08/25/lifestyle/chivalrous-men-cheat-as-much-as-misogynists-and-more-women-need-to-know-that-study/

6 White supremacy refers to the paradigm in which having lighter skin positions people as superior to those with darker skin. Whiteness grants people more status, privilege and safety than those with darker skin. White supremacy is connected to the racism that exists at all levels of society, including in smaller interactions in our personal relationships.

7 Misogyny refers to hatred, prejudice and discrimination toward non-men, usually expressed by men, but it can be internalized by anyone of any gender. Misogyny connects with the effects of male-dominated society, or patriarchy.

8 Cisgender refers to people who identify with the gender they were assigned at birth. For example, if a baby were born and the doctor declared, "It's a girl!" and this person grew up feeling like a girl and went on to identify as a woman, she would be a cisgender woman.

9 As a therapist, I really appreciate attachment theory as a tool for understanding communication through conflict. Check out Jessica Fern's *Polysecure: Attachment, Trauma and Consensual Nonmonogamy* (Thornapple Press, 2020) for more on attachment theory.

10 NRE describes explosive "happy chemicals" that pump through our systems for the first three-ish months to two-ish years of a relationship.

11 If you're interested in the intersection between nonmonogamy and neurodiversity, check out Alyssa Gonzalez's book *Nonmonogamy and Neurodiversity* (Thornapple Press, 2023).

About the

More Than Two® Essentials Series

More Than Two Essentials is a series of books by Canadian authors on focused topics in nonmonogamy. It is curated by Eve Rickert, author of *More Than Two, Second Edition: Cultivating Nonmonogamous Relationships with Kindness and Integrity*.

Learn more at morethantwo.ca.

More from the

More Than Two® Essentials Series

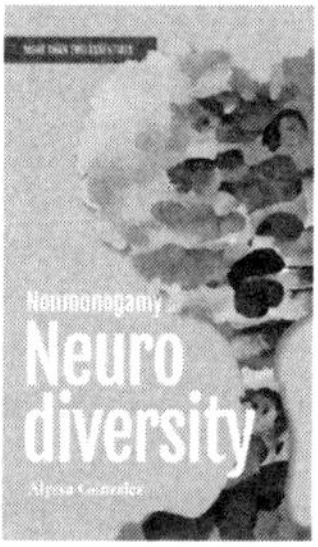

Nonmonogamy and Neurodiversity

Post-Nonmonogamy and Beyond

Nonmonogamy and Happiness

Nonmonogamy and Teaching

Marla Schreiber (MSW, RSW) is a white, Queer, gender-defiant, neurodivergent therapist and educator who has been practising polyamory since 2005. In their anti-oppressive, trauma-informed therapy work, Marla specializes in nonmonogamous relationships and 2SLGBTQIA+ identities. After designing and facilitating workshops and consulting in academic and professional settings, they founded the website PolyaMarla to offer nonmonogamy education.